Made in United States
North Haven, CT
14 March 2022

17142184R00085